Using Rubrics to Improve Student Writing

Kindergarten

REVISED EDITION

Sally Hampton

Sandra Murphy

Margaret Lowry

T 54864

The International Reading Association attempts, through its publications, to provide a forum for a wide spectrum of opinions on reading. This policy permits divergent viewpoints without implying the endorsement of the Association.

Executive Editor, Books	Corinne M. Mooney
Developmental Editor	Charlene M. Nichols
Developmental Editor	Tori Mello Bachman
Developmental Editor	Stacey L. Reid
Editorial Production Manager	Shannon T. Fortner
Design and Composition Manager	Anette Schuetz
Design and Production	Progressive Information Technologies

Cover photos: © 2008 Jupiterimages Corporation

The publisher would appreciate notification where errors occur so that they may be corrected in subsequent printings or editions.

Library of Congress Cataloging-in-Publication Data

Hampton, Sally.
   Using rubrics to improve student writing, kindergarten / Sally Hampton, Sandra Murphy, Margaret Lowry. — Rev. ed.
      p. cm.
   Includes bibliographical references.
   ISBN 978-0-87207-770-6
1. English language—Composition and exercises—Study and teaching (Early childhood)—United States—Evaluation.   2. Kindergarten—United States—Evaluation. I. Murphy, Sandra (Sandra M.) II. Lowry, Margaret (Margaret M.) III. Title.
   LB1139.5.L35H355 2009
   372.62'3044—dc22
                                                                2008030219

Contents

About the Authors

Sally Hampton is a Senior Fellow for America's Choice, Inc. Previously she served as Senior Scholar at the Carnegie Foundation for the Advancement of Teaching and as the Director of English Language Arts and Deputy Director of Research and Development for New Standards. She has taught in both urban and rural classrooms and developed reading and writing programs. Most recently she worked with Lauren Resnick to produce *Reading and Writing With Understanding*, a volume that addresses comprehension and composing in grades 4 and 5.

Sandra Murphy is a Professor Emerita at the University of California, Davis. She is interested particularly in writing assessment and its impact on teachers and curriculum, reading comprehension, and critical perspectives on literacy.

Margaret Lowry is the Director of First-Year English at the University of Texas at Arlington. She teaches courses in writing and U.S. literature and participates in the training of graduate teaching assistants. Her research interests include composition pedagogies, teacher training, and women's autobiographical writings.

About New Standards®

*N*ew Standards is a joint project of the Learning Research and Development Center at the University of Pittsburgh (Pennsylvania, USA) and The National Center on Education and the Economy (Washington, D.C., USA). From its beginning in 1991, New Standards was a leader in standards-based reform efforts. New Standards, heading a consortium of 26 U.S. states and 6 school districts, developed the New Standards® Performance Standards, a set of internationally competitive performance standards in English language arts, mathematics, science, and applied learning in grades 4, 8, and 10. New Standards also pioneered standards-based performance assessment, developing the New Standards® reference examinations and a portfolio assessment system to measure student achievement against the performance standards.

With support from the U.S. Department of Education, New Standards produced a collection of publications addressing literacy development, including the award-winning *Reading and Writing Grade by Grade*, as well as *Reading and Writing With Understanding*, *Speaking and Listening for Preschool Through Third Grade*, and a series on *Using Rubrics to Improve Student Writing* for kindergarten through fifth grade.

Preface

$\mathcal{W}$riting is hard work, and teaching children to write well is very hard work. Your commitment to this challenge is vital to the future success of all the students you teach, both while they are in school and later, when they become active members of their communities.

This book provides tools to help you teach writing. It contains information about written genres and specialized rubrics that emphasize writing strategies. It also includes a collection of student work with commentaries that explain the strengths and weaknesses of the examples.

Not all the student writing in this book is at standard. Instead, we have provided you with samples that are spread out along a continuum of performance, from work that is exceptional to work that falls considerably below what children at this grade level should be expected to produce. This continuum will allow you to identify similar performances from your students and let you see how far from—or close to—standard they are. The rubrics and commentaries have been designed to provide a formative assessment to help you plan instruction.

The students whose work is included here were fortunate to have been taught by dedicated professionals like you, teachers who helped them write with exuberance and purpose about what they knew, what they thought, what they wondered. They are novice writers, to be sure, but their potential is obvious in their ability to employ writing strategies and techniques to communicate with their audience.

We can all be guided and inspired by the work that follows.

Lauren B. Resnick
Codirector, New Standards
University of Pittsburgh

Marc S. Tucker
Codirector, New Standards
The National Center on Education and the Economy

Acknowledgments

The rubrics, student writing, and commentaries contained in this document were all compiled during the 2001–2002 school year. They were the result of work done in kindergarten through fifth-grade classrooms that used the New Standards® performance standards, the New Standards® Primary Literacy Standards, and America's Choice author and genre studies.

I would like to thank the many students, teachers, literacy coaches, and principals for their contribution to this document. The New Standards project acknowledges the work of the Noyce Foundation in the development of the rubrics.

Sally Hampton

Sally Hampton
Senior Fellow for Literacy
America's Choice, Inc.

Introduction

Formative Assessment in the Age of Accountability

In today's world, schools are being held accountable for student performance on state tests. Summative assessments of this kind provide useful information to the public and to policymakers. But the information they provide is of limited use to teachers, primarily because state assessment results arrive too late to effectively inform instruction. In this book we hope to help teachers develop an informed perspective about formative assessment and how that kind of assessment is an effective tool for instruction that fosters student learning.

There are clear differences between formative and summative assessments. Summative assessments sum up learning. They evaluate student performances in terms of where students are expected to be at the end of an instructional year or grading period.

Formative assessments, on the other hand, are intended to provide feedback and to guide instruction. Teachers who conduct formative assessments gather information about what their students know and are able to do at various points in time; using this information, they make decisions about what students need help with next. They also use this information to provide feedback to students. The best formative assessments, according to Paul Black and his colleagues, are those that provide effective feedback (see, for example, Black & Wiliam, 1998). Black describes the characteristics of such feedback as follows: First, effective feedback must be intelligible so that students can grasp its significance and use it both as a self-assessment tool and as a guide for improvement. Second, effective feedback must focus on particular qualities of the student's work. Third, effective feedback must provide advice about how to improve the work and set an achievable target. To these criteria we would add two caveats: First, effective feedback must evolve as students acquire new skills. Second, effective feedback about writing should not be generic; it should refer to particular genres and the elements and strategies associated with them.

Learning About Genres

A genre is a rough template for accomplishing a particular purpose with language. It provides the writer and the reader with a common set of assumptions about what characterizes the text. So, for example, if the text is labeled a mystery story, there is an assumption that the story line will be built around some puzzle to be resolved or some crime to be solved. Likewise, when a piece starts off "Once upon a time...," there is an assumption that we will be reading or writing a fairy tale or a parody of a fairy tale. But if the first line of a text is "Whales are mammals," we expect a very different genre—a report of information instead of a story.

As Charles Cooper (1999) explains, writers shape texts to accomplish different purposes by using and adapting particular patterns of organization, by using particular techniques to develop the text, and by making particular language choices. Although there is a lot of variation from one text to another within the same genre, texts in a particular genre nevertheless follow a general pattern. As a result, readers develop expectations that enable them to anticipate where a text is going so they can make sense of it as they read. Writers know how to order and present thoughts in language patterns readers can recognize and follow.

Lack of genre knowledge will impair a student's academic success. The student who is required to produce a report but who does not know the expectations relative to report writing is immediately disadvantaged. That student must guess at how information might be ordered, what kind of stance/persona could be effective, how much information should be provided, and what level of specificity would be sufficient. By comparison, the student who is genre savvy and is aware of the various expectations attached to informational writing can choose which genre expectations to guide his or her writing, which to disregard, and if or where to vary the conventional pattern. This genre-savvy student enjoys a tremendous advantage over the first student.

Genre knowledge also supports reading comprehension. If children are familiar with the structure of a text, they can make predictions and understand the functions of text features such as dialogue, and so read more purposefully. Moreover, being familiar with the text structure also makes it easier for readers to internalize the information in a text. Students who understand the organizational pattern of a text can use this knowledge to locate key information, identify what is important and unimportant, synthesize information that appears in different locations within a text, and organize the information in memory. In general, making readers more aware of genre structure appears to improve comprehension, memory, and, thus, learning.

Several genres are fundamental to writing development in kindergarten through fifth grade. The four that are discussed in this book and the others in the grade-by-grade New Standards rubrics series are (1) narrative writing (sharing events, telling stories), (2) report of information (informing others), (3) instructions (instructing others about how to get things done), and (4) responding to literature. The characteristic features of each of these genres are presented in rubrics that describe different levels of performance.

In their current form, the rubrics in this book are not designed to be used with students. They are too complex, and their language is too abstract for children. However, the rubrics can easily serve as templates for guiding the development of grade-level-appropriate classroom rubrics that address elements and strategies. They are, in effect, end-of-the-year targets from which a teacher maps backward to plan instruction.

What Makes a Rubric Good to Use With Students?

Rubrics can be developed and used in formative or summative ways. Typically, rubrics used in summative evaluation are short. They provide a minimum amount of detail so that scorers can quickly and efficiently assign a score to a piece of student writing. Rubrics used in summative assessment are also static, out of necessity. After all, only by using the same rubric can you get comparative data in order to report trends over time. Further,

they represent how students are expected to write at the end of a grading period. Summative rubrics don't provide information about the road along the way. Formative rubrics, on the other hand, trace patterns of development and focus on the particular.

Focus on the Particular

The brevity required for efficient scoring and the static nature of summative rubrics fight against what teachers and students need to foster writing development. For example, it is not enough for a writer to be told that his or her writing is "well organized," a phrase commonly found on generic rubrics in state assessments. Such a global statement does not help the writer understand what it takes to make writing well organized. A more effective descriptor would be, "Clearly sequences events in the story and maintains control of point of view."

Be Intelligible

Formative rubrics must also be meaningful to students. Ideally, they should grow out of the work of the classroom and represent a consensus about what constitutes good writing. They must be written in language that the students understand, language that is familiar. The goal is for students to be able to self-assess their writing in order to take on productive revisions and interact with peers in response groups or with the teacher in a conference. The language of the rubric should frame such interactions so that they are meaningful to everyone and grounded in the classroom culture.

Set Targets and Offer Advice

Formative rubrics should set targets and offer advice. At each score level, a good rubric provides a list of criteria that defines performance at that level. Advancement to the next level (the target) comes about by refining the paper to match the criteria in the next score level. So, for example, if a student's paper is at score point 2 and that student wants a score point 3, the student must revise the paper to include all the elements for the higher score currently missing from the paper or must refine the way in which the elements and strategies in his or her paper are developed. Rubrics are not good tools for revision if the distinctions between score levels are set only by qualifiers such as "scant" detail, "some" detail, "adequate" detail, and "effective" detail. Better rubrics provide more definitive distinctions: "no introduction," "an introduction that names the topic and provides at least minimal context," or "an introduction that names the topic, provides context, and generates reader interest." Better rubrics focus on the features and components of particular genres (for example, in narrative, character development, plot, dialogue, flashback). Such rubrics provide students and teachers with language to talk about the ways certain texts accomplish particular purposes. The rubrics presented in this book encompass both the genre elements and the strategies associated with each genre.

Be Developed in a Classroom Setting

Students and teachers need formative rubrics that emerge from the teaching in a classroom and that specify work yet to be done. To learn about genres, students need to be engaged in active inquiry. Guided by their teachers, they can analyze texts of a published author, a peer, or their own work, and develop classroom rubrics as they examine the texts. The texts will serve as examples and inspiration. These classroom rubrics should be constructed as guidelines to improve student writing performance.

When rubrics are constructed as guidelines to improve performance, it is possible for a student, working alone or with a teacher, to use a rubric as a checklist—a rough approximation of what is in place and how well wrought these elements are. Once that is done, the student should be able to study the criteria at the next level to determine what further work would need to be done for the writing to show significant improvement.

The above is an example of a classroom rubric, constructed jointly by a teacher and her students. This joint construction ensures a shared understanding about what constitutes good writing and about what "next steps" should guide instruction. The sample text at the bottom of this rubric was composed jointly by the teacher and her students. This is an end-of-year rubric, so the students could all read the criteria.

In some cases, such as when papers are almost at standard, a simple revision by the student is enough to sufficiently improve the quality of the work. The revision conference would have the teacher providing a reminder, such as, "Did you forget x?" or a suggestion, "Could you tell me more about the main character? For instance, what color is his hair?" No instruction would be necessary; the writer would just need to be nudged a bit. But in other cases, to bring the paper "up to standard" would require significantly more than a nudge. Many papers signal a substantial need for instruction, time, and practice.

Note: Implicit here are two assumptions. One, that it is the job of the teacher to enable the writer and not just "fix" the paper. And two, that learning to write takes time. In some cases, learning to use the elements that define the next higher score point might take up to a year!

Change With Instruction

Formative rubrics grow. Thoughtful teachers know that they have to move students from their initial performances in September to more refined performances at the end of the year. The instruction they provide will make this change possible. Consider the kindergarten students who begin school with no awareness of the conventions of print. When asked to write a story, they will likely draw a picture and perhaps include some random letters. After instruction, and with time, these students will begin to produce writing that moves from left to right, and top to bottom. They likely will copy words from word charts and play with phonetic spelling. Initial rubrics should celebrate this growth with criteria aimed at moving students forward one step at a time.

Older students, too, will improve with focused instruction and practice. Consider a beginning of the year third-grade classroom in which a teacher is doing a study on narration. The first rubric might have as few as three elements in order to represent what students initially know:

1. Has a beginning that interests the reader
2. Has a number of events that taken together tell a story
3. Has some sort of closure

The three-element rubric captures the essence of narrative and, hence, is complete. A more fully developed narrative rubric would also have some mention of transitions and probably some mention of detail. So, the rubric could easily grow from three to five descriptors, as the teacher provides the necessary instruction.

Growing a Rubric

Changing the Number of Levels

Just as the number of descriptors in a rubric may grow, so may the number of levels. Assume the teacher begins the year with a rubric that has three levels: meets the standard, "great writing"; approaches the standard, "O.K. writing"; and needs more work, "ready for revision." As fewer students produce work that falls below standard, the bottom distinctions can disappear (literally be removed/cut off/marked out). Then what was once work that "meets the standard" can become "approaching a higher standard." This can be determined by teacher and students collaboratively. Similarly, work that "met the standard" can now become "ready for revision." Growing a rubric like this—constantly reexamining how good work must be to earn the highest distinction—is a powerful way to highlight student *growth* in writing.

Changing the Anchor Papers

In themselves, rubrics leave much room for ambiguity. They can be made more explicit by providing examples of what they describe. These examples are called *anchor* papers. When the words on the rubric remain unchanged, but the paper that illustrates the level of performance they describe changes, the rubric is said to be "recalibrated." An example will help here: Assume that the rubric simply states, "has a beginning that engages the reader." The paper that initially illustrates that concept may have a simple opening sentence/phrase ("Once upon a time there lived a king" or "On Saturday, I saw light"). If recalibrated, the anchor paper would provide a more complex beginning, for example: a paragraph or longer that sets a plot in motion, an example of dialogue that immediately creates reader interest, a description that is simply riveting (think of the beginning of *Maniac McGee*), or even the resolution of a story told as a flashback.

Understanding These Rubrics

Elements and Strategies

The rubrics in this book are divided into two parts. The first section delineates the elements that are fundamental to the genre, and the second section lays out the strategies writers frequently employ to enhance the genre.

This division of the rubric is intentional. The elements are of critical importance and are foundational to the genre. Until a writer can address the elements with some proficiency, an instructional focus on strategies is misguided. Yet, it is not unusual for instruction to skip from very basic work on introductions and conclusions to an emphasis on lifting the level of language in a piece, most often by inserting metaphors and similes. While figurative language can distinguish a good piece of writing, it cannot compensate for a fundamental lack of development. Think of the compulsories in an Olympic figure skating event. The skater must demonstrate proficiency performing the athletic stunts required by the judges before attempting the more creative dance moves that are also part of his or her repertoire. Genres, likewise, require the writer to address certain elements.

That is not to say that the strategies are unimportant. Frequently, they work with the elements to carry a reader through the text. Consider the work of dialogue in advancing the plot of a novel. The dialogue provides clues about who characters are and what motivates them. Dialogue also frequently helps a reader make transitions when there are scene changes or shifts in time. But a novel without a well-developed plot, well-developed characters, or some organizational frame will not be made whole simply with the inclusion of dialogue.

Too often, writing instruction in narrative focuses on leads and transitions to structure chronological ordering and on teaching strategies out of context (for instance, including dialogue for the sake of having dialogue, rather than as a strategy to develop character or advance the action). In many classrooms, not enough time is spent on the elements, the "compulsories" of genres. For this reason, the rubrics have been designed to emphasize both strategies and elements. When teachers use the rubrics to analyze students' strengths and weaknesses in order to plan instruction, they should first focus on the elements section. The strategies can be folded in instructionally as students begin to demonstrate awareness of the elements. In some cases, young writers will likely pick up strategies on their own through their reading and by appropriating text from favorite authors.

Note: The lists of elements and strategies provided in these materials are foundational. They are not meant to be exhaustive or exclusive.

For grades 1 to 5, the rubrics have five levels. At kindergarten, however, we suggest using only three. This difference grows out of respect for the developmental differences of kindergarten children, who enter school at as much as a 12-month range of ages and with diverse backgrounds and experiences at home and in preschool settings. Further, for a growing number of children, kindergarten is a full-day program, but half-day kindergarten is still the norm for many.

Kindergarten work at score point 3 exceeds the standard; at score point 2, meets the standard; and at score point 1, approaches the standard. Because kindergarten writing depends very much on the experiences and maturity that a child brings to the classroom, the criteria for score points 3 and 2 are not identical (as they are for score points 5 and 4 in the higher grades). It is likely that students who have attended preschool and who have been read to extensively will take to writing much more easily than those who have not had such experiences. They will often be better able to handle directionality and sound–letter correspondences, and they will be more fluent on paper. These factors account for the differences between score points 3 and 2.

Students who produce work at score point 1 need more time and instruction to write at standard, but there is not necessarily the same need for substantial support as might be the case for students in the higher grades who produce work at the lowest score point. It may simply be the case that kindergarten students who do not produce writing at standard do so because of age differences or lack of time in the classroom.

How to Use These Rubrics

Research, as well as practical experience, demonstrate that within any single classroom, the range of performance in writing and in children's knowledge of genre is wide. In any particular grade, some students' papers will look like the work of children in earlier grades, whereas the work of other students will appear more advanced. Even the work of a single child will show great variation from day to day because development does not progress smoothly forward in step-by-step increments. Moreover, skills that appear to be mastered are sometimes thrown into disarray as new skills are acquired.

We also know that students write some genres better than others. Research shows that young children typically have more experience with narrative genres than scientific or poetic genres. Research also shows that children are more successful handling the familiar structure of stories than the less familiar structure of arguments. One explanation for these differences may lie in the instruction about genres children receive, or do not receive, in school. Another explanation may be related to their experiences outside of school. If children have had infrequent exposure to particular genres, they will be less adept at writing and reading them than children who have had frequent exposure.

To use these rubrics, a teacher should first ask each student to produce a piece of writing specific to a particular genre. If the genre is narrative, the teacher might say, "I'd like you to write a story about...." If the genre is informational, the teacher might say, "I'd like you to write a report about...." If the genre is instructional writing, "I'd like you to write a paper explaining how to do something." Or if the genre is response to literature, "I'd like you to read this story/book/poem [or at kindergarten, "I'd like you to listen as I read"] and then write a paper that explains what the author is saying."

Once the student writing is in hand, the teacher should analyze individual performances with the appropriate genre rubric. This analysis will indicate what kinds of instruction are needed for students to gain the knowledge and skills required to produce work in that genre at score point 2 (meets the standard).

Note: Making a judgment about proficiency on the basis of a single sample is always chancy. To have a better sense of a student's proficiency, it is always wise to look at several samples.

It is almost certain that student work will not reflect the same level of proficiency for each element and strategy contained in the rubric. That is, a student writer may establish a strong orientation and context (score point 3), but develop character only weakly (score point 1). The student could make good use of dialogue (score point 2), but provide too few details (score point 1). In fact, most papers produced by novice writers are of this uneven quality.

The point of these rubrics is not to assign an overall score to student work, as one might do in a formal assessment, and certainly not to assign a grade. Rather, it is to highlight for teachers the characteristics of student work at different levels of performance so that appropriate instruction and feedback can be provided. Grading student writing is a necessity for teachers, and it is essential that the grades assigned reflect student performance relative to the genre elements and strategies. Grades can be derived from the classroom rubric. See the sample classroom rubric on page 3.

How to Use the Papers and Commentary

Papers at each score point are representative of what work at that score level might look like. They are concrete examples of what the rubric describes. The commentaries describe the student writing in relation to the rubric. Teachers can use the papers and commentaries to calibrate the levels of performance of their own students. Comparing their students' work with the work in this book will highlight for teachers the various levels of proficiency among their students and facilitate instructional planning. Students in upper-elementary grades can study the papers as models of work that represent either a strong performance for a genre or work that could be strengthened through revision. Teachers can use the commentaries to scaffold discussion, and working together, teachers and students can construct classroom rubrics. A further use for the papers and commentaries is as the focus for teacher meetings where the goal is to establish a shared understanding of what good writing looks like.

In all cases, the commentaries have been written with the intention of honoring what is in place in the papers. Too often, student assessment focuses entirely on what is missing and/or what is poorly done. This genre-based approach to writing assumes that writing development is a layered process in which new learning builds over time upon what is already in place. The starting point is always first to identify the paper's strengths. In this manner, writing assessment is a positive, additive process, one that is also transparent and meaningful to students.

At the end of each of the commentaries for papers at score point 1, there is a set of "next-step" suggestions. These next-step suggestions are simply that—suggestions. It may well be that other sets of suggestions could also work. However, the suggestions provided were drawn from an analysis of dozens of papers typical of that score point, as well as from an analysis of the particular paper described in the commentary.

It should be emphasized that students at score point 2 and score point 1 will take time and practice to improve. There will be some slow steps forward and some backsliding on the students' part. But these are novice writers, so patience, practice, and coaching should be part of any instructional plan.

This book has been designed with insight into the complexities of teaching writing. It includes student work as models and lists of rubric criteria as scales, two things that, according to George Hillocks (1984), research indicates will improve student writing if used appropriately. This book was drawn from the work of dedicated teachers and hard-working students. (To protect their privacy, names have been removed.) Admittedly, this is only one part of a comprehensive writing program, but it will serve well those teachers who use it to plan for student instruction.

The student papers in this book were chosen from more than 5,000 pieces written by students in many different elementary schools in several different school districts. The papers illustrate the range of abilities and performance of students at different grade levels from kindergarten through fifth grade, as well as ranges within grade levels. In the first year of the project, 3,586 students participated. Their teachers taught author and genre studies, and at the end of the year, the teachers collected portfolios of student writing. The examples in this book are drawn from these students' portfolios.

Narrative

Narrative is the genre most commonly associated with elementary schools. In fact, people assume that narrative, or more specifically, story, is the purview of our youngest students. To a large extent this assumption is logical. Elementary school is filled with story—picture books, show and tell, dramas, and basal readers. Children make sense of their lives and their worlds through story. Jerome Bruner (1985) tells us, "They [young children] are not able to…organize things in terms of cause and effect and relationships, so they turn things into stories, and when they try to make sense of their life they use the storied version of their experience as the basis for further reflection. If they don't catch something in a narrative structure, it doesn't get remembered very well, and it doesn't seem to be accessible for further kinds of mulling over."

Narratives have time as their deep structure. A narrative involves a series of events that can be plotted out on some sort of time line. The time span could be short, a few moments, or long, even across generations.

There are many kinds of narratives (frequently called subgenres): memoirs, biographies, accounts, anecdotes, folktales, recounts, mysteries, autobiographies, etc. Recount is a kind of narrative in which the teller simply retells events for the purpose of informing or entertaining. Anecdotes, on the other hand, generally include some kind of crisis that generates an emotional reaction—frustration, satisfaction, insecurity, etc. Stories, in contrast, exhibit a somewhat different pattern. A complication creates a problem, which then has to be overcome (the resolution). Stories are built of events that are causally linked (the events recounted share a cause–effect relationship). Think for a moment about stories. It is quite easy to say of them, "this happened because this happened, so this happened and that caused this to happen."

Narrative accounts, by contrast, are comprised of a series of events that in total may or may not add up to anything significant other than the reader's sense of "this is how things went." It is a matter of "this happened and then this and then this and then this." Folktales take yet another form. Like other genres, different subgenres of narrative can serve different purposes, for example, to entertain or to make a point about what people should do, or about how the world should be.

The New Standards expectation for student writers around narrative requires that they be able to craft a narrative account, either fiction or nonfiction, that does the following: establishes a context; creates a point of view; establishes a situation or plot; creates an organizing structure; provides detail to develop the event sequence and characters; uses a range of appropriate strategies, such as dialogue; and provides closure.

Orientation and Context

As it relates to narrative, orienting the reader and providing context usually involves bringing readers into the narrative (situating them somehow in the story line) and engaging them.

There are many ways to do this, of course, but among the most common strategies are

- Introducing a character who is somehow interesting
- Establishing a situation that intrigues or startles a reader
- Situating a reader in a time and place
- Having a narrator speak directly to the reader in order to create empathy or interest

From this initial grounding, writers can begin to develop the event sequence of their narratives.

Plot Development and Organization

The organization of narrative is not necessarily a straightforward chronological ordering of events. Consider just a few variations. Narratives frequently are organized as the simultaneously ongoing, unfolding of events in the lives of multiple persons or fictional characters. The end of such a narrative requires that several or all of these persons' or characters' lives come together. In some narratives, the sequence of events may be altered to create interest, so the writer may use flashbacks and flash-forwards to move the characters around in time or to create a "backstory" of the events leading up to the story. Stories within a story are another commonly used device. Mystery stories often are organized by laying out an initiating event (crime), and then providing a series of clues and several false resolutions before the truth is finally revealed. Newspaper stories traditionally flow from the standard "who, what, where, when, why, how?" of an introductory paragraph. Memoir is organized around a single event or series of events that sum up the essence of who someone is, or was, and what values and heritage shaped that person. Biography and autobiography usually begin with birth and move through early years, adolescent years, and late years of someone's life. The diversity of narrative genres, as well as the myriad ways in which they can be developed, serve to remind us of the various options writers have for communicating with readers.

In general, however, narratives are often organized in such a way that some event precipitates a causally linked series of further events, which in some way is ultimately resolved. Episodes share a relationship to each other and usually are built around a problem and emotional response, an action, and an outcome. Nuanced plotting frequently involves subplots, built through episodes, and shifts in time. The classic plot structures for conflict are man vs. man, man vs. society, man vs. nature, and man vs. self.

Although children and adults may tell complicated narratives, it is important to remember that they also tell simple recounts. Recounts tell what happened, and organization is based on a series of events that all relate to a particular occasion. Children often recount personal narratives about school excursions or particularly memorable events in their lives—their immigration to America, the death of a cherished pet, the birth of a sister, and so on. In recounts, sometimes there is not an initiating event; rather, writers present a bed-to-bed story that retells the mundane events of the day.

Adult writers use a variety of methods to develop event sequences and their settings. They typically develop settings by providing details about place, colors, structures, landscape, and so on. They use several techniques to manage event sequences and time, including flashbacks and flash-forwards, forecasting, and back stories. They sometimes manipulate time by compressing or expanding it, that is, by providing pacing. They use dialogue and possibly interior monologue purposefully to advance the action. During the elementary school years, children are just beginning to master these techniques.

Because narratives are based on events in time, writers also often use linking words that deal with time and the organization of events (then, before, after, when, while). When people recount events, they often refer to the specific times when events happened (yesterday, last summer). As children mature, their repertoire of temporal signals develops, from simple transition words (then, after, before) to more complex phrases ("At the time…") and clauses ("Before he went in the house…").

Character/Narrator Development

Adult writers use a variety of techniques to develop characters, and in some cases, the persona of the narrator. They describe their physical characteristics, their personalities, their actions and gestures, their emotional reactions to events, and through dialogue and internal monologue, their internal motivations and goals. Whether narratives include real people or fictional characters, the personalities, motivations, and reactions of the narrator and the characters are often central to the development of the narrative. When children develop characters, some are "stock characters" that regularly inhabit children's stories, such as the mean teacher, the school bully, and the wicked witch. Other characters are more fully and uniquely developed through description, dialogue, and other narrative techniques.

Although children may produce narratives in which fictional characters are fairly well developed, they are less likely to develop the persona of the narrator. And, when they are producing simple recounts of events in their lives, neither the people in their narrative nor the persona of the narrator may be particularly well developed. In simple recounts, the focus is more likely to be on what people did than on their motives or reactions.

Closure

Writers bring closure to narratives in a variety of ways. Structurally, they achieve closure by providing a resolution to a problem (or a failed resolution). But they also provide closure with a variety of overt signals—with evaluations that inform the reader what the narrator thought about the events, with comments that serve to tie up loose ends in the narrative or bridge the gap between the narrative and the present, and with typical ending markers such as "the end" and "they all lived happily ever after." As children mature, their strategies for providing closure become more sophisticated and their repertoire of strategies more broad.

Narrative in Kindergarten

Children enter kindergarten with widely different levels of preparedness for becoming literate. At this time in their lives, most children are in the beginning stages of literacy development. Some of them may not yet be writing texts that can be understood by others. Their "writing" may consist of drawings (pictures can represent events), "scribbling," or writing via letter-like forms. Some children may only reveal their knowledge of genres through oral language, in activities such as story time, in retellings, in dictation, and

the like. Other children may come to school with a running start, already reading and writing. For the most part, the samples in this book are from children who have progressed beyond that earliest stage of learning and who are writing texts that can be understood by others (via their phonetic spellings or conventional English orthography). But even for these children, the range of performance in any single classroom is very wide.

When writing personal narratives, some children in kindergarten may relate only a single incident or action, such as a narrative with a simple beginning and end ("I wi to the prc [I went to the park] I paD wIth CAT [I played with a cat] I Wu PAE [I love to play]"). They may provide little, if any, character development, and few details. They may not provide closure to their writing.

Students who meet the standard for narrative writing demonstrate an emerging grasp of context. For instance, they may establish a place ("I went to Disnand [Disneyland]"), but not establish a time. Other writers may establish both ("I went to balens parke on Sunday."). They are able to control for chronological ordering in their narratives. They create narratives that are made up of several incidents, although the incidents are usually only loosely linked together. These narratives are often simple recountings of "what happened" with one event strung after another ("I wac up and I gitt jest [get dressed] and I mac a haf of a phit budri [peanut butter] and jelle sanwis [jelly sandwich] and I prt it in my big [bag]..."). Writers who meet the standard provide a sense of closure to their narratives, and they may conclude with a simple reflection. They may include drawings that support meaning.

Narrative Rubrics Elements

	3 **Exceeds Standard**	**2** **Meets Standard**	**1** **Approaching Standard**
Orientation and Context	• Demonstrates an emerging grasp of context (e.g., time and place).	• Demonstrates an emerging grasp of context (e.g., time and place).	• Demonstrates an emerging grasp of context (e.g., time and place).
Plot Development and Organization	• Creates a "story" or recount made up of several incidents or actions, some of which may be loosely linked. • Controls for chronological ordering.	• Creates a "story" or recount made up of several incidents or actions, some of which may be loosely linked. • Controls for chronological ordering.	• May have some sort of "story" or recount in picture or words, typically a single incident or action.
Character/ Narrator Development	• Provides little, if any, character development.	• Provides little, if any, character development.	• Provides little, if any, character development.
Closure	• Provides a sense of closure (e.g., a simple reflection or "THE END.").	• May provide a sense of closure.	• Typically does not provide a sense of closure.

Narrative Rubrics Strategies

	3 **Exceeds Standard**	**2** **Meets Standard**	**1** **Approaching Standard**
Detail	• Uses details to describe incidents and people.	• Uses details to describe incidents and people.	• Uses few details.
Dialogue	• May attempt dialogue (e.g., "Then the Dockter said shes ok").	• Typically does not attempt dialogue.	• Typically does not attempt dialogue.
Other	• May use simple transition words (e.g., and, then). • May use drawings to expand or illustrate the text.	• May use simple transition words (e.g., "and," "then"). • May use drawings to expand or illustrate the text.	• Typically does not use transition words. • May use drawings to expand or illustrate the text.

Score Point 3

Narrative Student Work and Commentary: "I wac uP and I gitt jeSt..."

I wac uP and I gitt
jeSt and I Mac a haf
of a Pnit Budn and
Jlie Sanwis and I prt it
in my big and then I mac
the weSdi of My Lus and
tan my mom Comz my heL.

This is an exceptional piece—it exceeds the standard for end-of-the-year kindergarten writing. In this piece, the young writer tells the story of what is involved in getting ready for school and beginning the school day. The piece reads like a "bed-to-bed" narrative in that the writer creates no center or distinguishing event; that is, there is no attempt to distinguish between what is and is not important. One event simply follows another and there is no attempt to establish a context. Nonetheless, the number of events sequenced is quite impressive.

The opening sentence ("I wac uP and I gitt jeSt") does not create a specific context for readers, but it does indicate a plan about where to begin the narrative.

The writer creates a story about getting ready for school in the morning, and she recounts several actions that she takes to get ready (get dressed, make lunch, comb hair, eat breakfast, wait for mommy, go to school, walk in line). The writer includes several events, and they are ordered appropriately.

The final sentence provides a sense of closure by summing up the writer's feelings about going to school ("I like scill.").

The writer includes an impressive number of details: making half of a peanut butter sandwich, eating toast for breakfast, going to school "wif my sibing's," walking "in lin" with the class, and sitting "on the copnt."

The final page includes a picture of the teacher and the children in the classroom.

The writer attempts dialogue in the piece ("MrS. --- sas grd Mroing"), and she uses transition words that indicate a temporal connection ("and then").

Score Point 3 continued

②

And then I et my befis.
and I had tost for befisd
And then I'n wetedy and
then I wat for mommy
and wen mommy is wen E
and we got to wif my Sibings.
and wen wer at sol I.
git in Lin and I wat

③

for Mrs   we wac
in Lin   to oL cas
wrm   we et bt Scf
uwry   we Sid dan
on the   copnt Mrs
        grd mroing and
then we diL the cawid
and I like salt

Score Point 3 *continued*

Score Point 3 continued

Assessment Summary: "I wac uP and I gitt jeSt..."

ELEMENTS		
	Exceeds Standard	**Commentary**
Orientation and Context	• Demonstrates an emerging grasp of context (e.g., time and place).	The opening sentence ("I wac uP and I gitt jeSt") does not create a specific context for readers, but it does indicate a plan about where to begin the narrative.
Plot Development and Organization	• Creates a "story" or recount made up of several incidents or actions, some of which may be loosely linked. • Controls for chronological ordering.	The writer creates a story about getting ready for school in the morning, and she recounts several actions that she takes to get ready (get dressed, make lunch, comb hair, eat breakfast, wait for mommy, go to school, walk in line). The writer includes several events, and they are ordered appropriately.
Character/ Narrator Development	• Provides little, if any, character development.	
Closure	• Provides a sense of closure (e.g., a simple reflection or "THE END.").	The final sentence provides a sense of closure by summing up the writer's feelings about going to school ("I like scill.").
STRATEGIES		
	Exceeds Standard	**Commentary**
Detail	• Uses details to describe incidents and people.	The writer includes an impressive number of details: making half of a peanut butter sandwich, eating toast for breakfast, going to school "wif my sibing's," walking "in lin" with the class, and sitting "on the copnt."
Dialogue	• May attempt dialogue (e.g., "Then the Dockter said shes ok").	The writer attempts dialogue in the piece ("MrS. --- sas grd Mroing").
Other	• May use simple transition words (e.g., and, then). • May use drawings to expand or illustrate the text.	The piece includes transition words that indicate a temporal connection ("and then"). The final page includes a picture of the teacher and the children in the classroom.

Note: The commentary highlights the elements and strategies in the student paper, focusing on how well the paper addresses the totality of the elements and strategies rather than on whether each is included.

Score Point 2

Narrative Student Work and Commentary:
"I went tOb balens parke..."

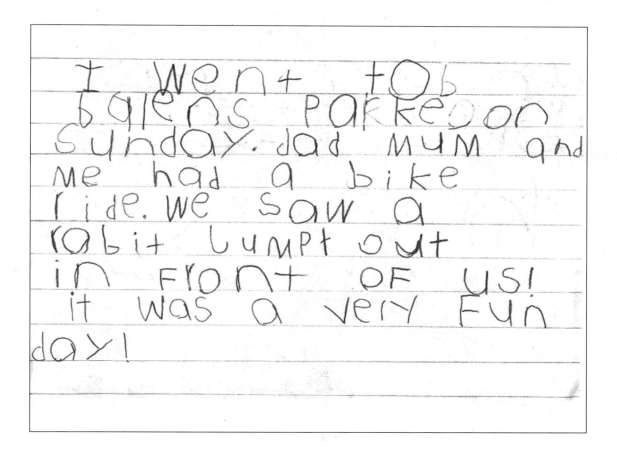

I went tOb balens parke on sunday. dad mum and me had a bike ride. we saw a rabit lumpt out in front of us! it was a very fun day!

This piece is representative of end-of-year kindergarten writing. It has an initiating event followed by subsequent activities, and the writer concludes the piece with a reflection. This piece is actually a variant on the familiar "I went to the park. It was fun," but the writer moves beyond that simple formula by providing a significant amount of detail.

The writer begins the piece by providing a sense of place and time ("I went tOb balens parke on Sunday.").

The initiating event (going to the park) is followed by two subsequent events (riding bikes with his parents and seeing a rabbit).

The piece includes a reflection that provides a sense of closure ("it was a very fun day!").

The piece includes some detail ("it jumpt OUt in Front OF US!").

The piece includes a drawing that illustrates the story.

Score Point 2 *continued*

Score Point 2 *continued*

Assessment Summary:
"I went tOb balens parke..."

ELEMENTS		
	Meets Standard	**Commentary**
Orientation and Context	• Demonstrates an emerging grasp of context (e.g., time and place).	The writer begins the piece by providing a sense of place and time ("I went tOb balens parke on Sunday.").
Plot Development and Organization	• Creates a "story" or recount made up of several incidents or actions, some of which may be loosely linked. • Controls for chronological ordering.	The initiating event (going to the park) is followed by two subsequent events (riding bikes with his parents and seeing a rabbit).
Character/ Narrator Development	• Provides little, if any, character development.	
Closure	• May provide a sense of closure.	The piece includes a reflection that provides a sense of closure ("it was a very fun day!").

STRATEGIES		
	Meets Standard	**Commentary**
Detail	• Uses details to describe incidents and people.	The piece includes some detail ("it jumpt OUt in Front OF US!").
Dialogue	• Typically does not attempt dialogue.	
Other	• May use simple transition words (e.g., and, then). • May use drawings to expand or illustrate the text.	The piece includes a drawing that illustrates the story.

Note: The commentary highlights the elements and strategies in the student paper, focusing on how well the paper addresses the totality of the elements and strategies rather than on whether each is included.

$\mathcal{S}$core $\mathcal{P}$oint **1**

Narrative Student Work and Commentary:
"go To MS --- KAS FIeAd..."

This is a very nice piece of kindergarten writing about the events that happen during a school day. The piece approaches, but does not meet, the standard for narrative.

The first sentence demonstrates an emerging grasp of context by describing what the writer does every day ("go To MS --- KAS FIeAd [every day]. ").

The writer recounts some of the classroom activities (made a book, spelled words, and counted chairs).

The writer concludes the piece by explaining that she went to another teacher's class.

The piece includes a drawing that illustrates the story.

Score Point 1 continued

Assessment Summary: "go To MS --- KAS FleAd..."

ELEMENTS		
	Approaching Standard	**Commentary**
Orientation and Context	• Demonstrates an emerging grasp of context (e.g., time and place).	The first sentence demonstrates an emerging grasp of context by describing what the writer does every day ("go To MS --- KAS FleAd [every day].").
Plot Development and Organization	• May have some sort of "story" or recount in picture or words, typically a single incident or action.	The writer recounts some of the classroom activities (made a book, spelled words, and counted chairs).
Character/ Narrator Development	• Provides little, if any, character development.	
Closure	• Typically does not provide a sense of closure.	The writer concludes the piece by explaining that she went to another teacher's class.
STRATEGIES		
	Approaching Standard	**Commentary**
Detail	• Uses few details.	
Dialogue	• Typically does not attempt dialogue.	
Other	• Typically does not use transition words. • May use drawings to expand or illustrate the text.	The piece includes a drawing that illustrates the story.

Note: The commentary highlights the elements and strategies in the student paper, focusing on how well the paper addresses the totality of the elements and strategies rather than on whether each is included.

Next Steps in Instruction

The writer will benefit from instruction on adding details about the activities in the day and providing a sense of closure.

Report of Information

Reports of information describe the way things are in the social and natural world. They describe classes of things, but also the components or parts of things and their relations. Reports contain various kinds of information. They answer questions such as, What are the major food groups? What is the earth made of? What role do planets play in the solar system? Reports also give information about aspects of things. They answer questions about size (How big is Texas? How tall is the Eiffel Tower?), about function (What is a telescope used for? What is a modem used for?), about behavior (What do pelicans do to find food? How do whales eat?), and about the organization of systems (What is the relationship of the House to the Senate? How is the court system organized?). Writers of this genre typically make meaning by describing and classifying things and their distinctive features. For children, this often means writing about the features of different kinds of dinosaurs, insects, planes, pets, whales, and so on. When children study science, their reports may deal with different kinds of energy, different kinds of clouds, different types of cells, etc.

Report writing poses many challenges for young students. Writing about a topic that they know well presents a different set of challenges than writing about a topic that is unfamiliar. When students know the topic, organizing the information is the primary task that consumes their energy. When they do not know the topic, gathering and phrasing the information present additional challenges.

When students are writing about a topic they are familiar with, they can convey information in their own words and cluster information in categories that make sense to them. When they do not know the topic, they may not have the breadth or depth of understanding to analyze and categorize the information effectively. In these cases, young writers often seem to rely almost solely on headers, provided either by the teacher or by the reference materials themselves, to organize their writing.

When students do not know the topic, simply phrasing the information can be a daunting task. They must explain new information that they may not fully understand. So the logical thing for them to do is to borrow heavily from the wording in reference books to make sure they convey correctly the ideas they are writing about. Logically, then, the syntactic patterns that emerge under these circumstances frequently are made up of some introductory, transitional, or evaluative phrasings that string together word-for-word borrowings from reference books. This is called "patch" writing and it is particularly acceptable and expected in the primary grades, where students are encouraged to mimic the language of written texts, to apprentice themselves to authors, and to borrow stylistic techniques they observe professional writers using.

The New Standards expectation for student writers in the report genre requires that they be able to craft a report that does the following: establishes a context; creates an organizing structure appropriate to audience and purpose; communicates ideas, insights, or theories that are illustrated through facts, details, quotations, statistics, and other information; uses a range of appropriate strategies to develop the text; and provides closure.

Orientation and Context

As it relates to report writing, orienting the reader usually means providing some kind of opening statement locating the subject of the paper in the universe of things. For children, the opening statement often takes the form of a definition or classification (for instance, "Whales are mammals."). Alternatively, opening statements will sometimes provide an overview of the topic (for instance, "There are many different types of whales in the ocean.") or a comment on the organization of a system (for instance, "There are three branches in the government of the United States."). Young writers also often attempt to engage reader interest in the topic by introducing startling facts or by appealing to the reader in some fashion.

Organization of Information

In reports, facts are often grouped into topic areas in a hierarchical pattern of organization such as classification. Reports also describe patterns of relations among concepts linked to facts. Although reports are often considered neutral and voiceless, in reality they convey human agendas or points of view. Thus, effective reports have a controlling idea or perspective that contributes to the organization and coherence of the text. That is, information is selected and ordered in a way that contributes to the development of the idea. Organizing information in a report also requires writers to attend to the needs of their audience by providing the background information a reader would need to understand subsequent portions of the text. Writers also use paragraphing, subheads, transition words, and phrases and clauses to organize the information.

Development and Specificity of Information

There is a wide variety of ways to report information. Writers define things ("Corn is a vegetable."), give examples ("Dogs are man's best friend. Guide dogs help blind people."), and provide reasons ("My mom works on computers…I know why, she's an engineer."). Writers also explain phenomena ("Atoms are the insides of crystals…. Crystals get flat faces because the atoms form regular patterns inside."). They compare ("Some crystals are like flowers."; "Gray rabbits look like ash and smoke.") and they contrast ("Some crystals grow from lava and some grow from sea salt."). They relate cause and effect ("We used to have a dog, but my dad left the door open and he ran out into the street."). They describe ("Dolphins have a sharp and pointed face."). They specify ("I learned a lot from doing this report. I learned about different types of dogs and breeds."). They evaluate ("All crystals are different and that's what makes them so wonderful."). The different strategies that writers use can vary from a single sentence to a chunk of text several sentences long.

In developing information in a report, effective writers provide adequate and specific information about the topic. They usually write in the present tense, and they exclude information that is extraneous or inappropriate. They communicate ideas, insights, and theories that are elaborated on or illustrated by facts, details, quotations, statistics, or other information. Their language is factual and precise, rather than general and non-specific. They use clear and precise descriptive language to convey distinctive features (such as shape, size, color), components (such as parts of a machine, players on a team), behaviors (such as behaviors of animals: birthing, mating, eating), uses (such as uses of soap: washing hair, washing clothes, washing cars). Frequently, writers use specialized vocabulary specifically related to the topic (such as "pride," "cubs," and "dominant male" in a paper about lion families).

Many young writers pick topics from their everyday lives that they are knowledgeable about and that lend themselves to everyday vocabulary (such as siblings, family members, the family dog). In these cases, the writing may appear less sophisticated than the writing of a student who has picked a topic that lends itself to the use of technical vocabulary. But when students work with less familiar topics, the language they use may not appear to be their own. Both situations, in their own way, make it difficult to accurately evaluate the writer's development. It is important to keep in mind, though, that young writers who are imitating the language of the books they read are in the process of making that language their own.

Closure

Although their reports may not always have a formal conclusion, as would be expected in the writing of adults, young writers typically provide some sort of closure, such as a shift from particular facts to some kind of general statement or claim about the topic ("Everything is an adventure when you have a passport. All you have to do is get one!").

Report of Information in Kindergarten

Generally, kindergarten writers delight in telling others about things. Nevertheless, some will have difficulty with this genre. Like the range of performance in narrative writing, the range of performance in report writing in any single classroom will be very wide. Although they may attempt to convey facts and information about a topic, some children may create only simple list-like structures with few facts and little, if any, internal coherence ("I read by My Self in the Living Room. I youz The red boock bag do You No What is My Favrit boock is? Is my Favrit boock is The eala book. Is Nise to read I Like boocks boock."). These less advanced writers may find it hard to know what to include and what to exclude, so they may include extraneous or unrelated information. They may not include a title or a concluding sentence.

More advanced students are able to gather and share information about a topic, maintain a focus, and exclude extraneous information. Some use organizing structures similar to those found in books they have read, grouping facts within simple beginning, middle, and end structures or imitating chapters like those found in picture books. They supply facts and information relevant to the topic ("Elephants are gray."; "She lays 60,000 eggs and only 2 or 3 of the babies can be a mom octopus.") and simple explanations ("There [their] wiskers [whiskers] help them sense."). They use pictures to illustrate or elaborate on their texts. For instance, in one of the student samples the statement "The butterfly drinks" is accompanied by a drawing of a butterfly drinking nectar from a flower.

Students who meet the standard at this grade level may rely on the title to announce the topic or announce it in the first sentence. They maintain a focus, staying on topic. They include facts and information specific to the topic, using common, everyday vocabulary. They may include a simple concluding sentence. If they use pictures, the pictures relate to the topic.

Report of Information Rubrics Elements

	3 Exceeds Standard	2 Meets Standard	1 Approaching Standard
Orientation and Context	• May announce the topic in the first sentence. • May rely on the title to announce the topic.	• May announce the topic in the first sentence. • May rely on the title to announce the topic.	• May announce the topic in the first sentence. • May not include a title.
Organization of Information	• Produces and maintains a focus with an organizational structure (e.g., beginning, middle, end; chapters; circle structure).	• Typically maintains a focus; stays on topic.	• May present information in a simple list.
Development and Specificity of Information	• Includes facts and information specific to the topic.	• Includes facts and information specific to the topic.	• Makes some attempt to convey facts and information about the topic. • Provides few facts. • May include extraneous information.
Closure	• May include a simple concluding sentence.	• May include a simple concluding sentence.	• May include a simple concluding sentence.

Report of Information Rubrics Strategies

	3 Exceeds Standard	2 Meets Standard	1 Approaching Standard
Names and Vocabulary	• Uses common, everyday vocabulary.	• Uses common, everyday vocabulary.	• Uses common, everyday vocabulary.
Other	• Pictures, if present, support the text.	• Pictures, if present, relate to the topic.	• Pictures, if present, may relate to the topic.

Score Point 3

Report of Information Student Work and Commentary: "The Rabbits Story"

Although the writer calls this piece a "story" in the title, "The Rabbits Story" is an example of a report of information that exceeds the standard. The piece demonstrates the writer's emerging knowledge of the differences between the genres of narrative and report.

The writer relies only on the title to introduce the topic.

Except for a narrative-like comment about the way her mother deals with their pet rabbit's tendency to chew on the carpet ("My mom is sometimes mad at my rabbit because she chews the carpet so we got a bathroom mat for her to chew on."), the writer shares information about her own rabbit, and rabbits in general, in the list-like structure that is typical of report at this age ("My rabbit is gray. My rabbit is

friendly."). The details are not clustered by topic, but the piece has a general beginning, middle, and end.

The piece includes specific details and a simile to describe rabbits of different colors and to provide details about rabbit anatomy ("Gray rabbits lok like ash and smoke."; "There wiskers help them sense and it helps Them."). The writer generalizes about rabbits by drawing on her own experience ("I like rabbits because rabbits are soft.").

The piece's final sentence is a statement about what rabbits eat ("Rabbits like carrots.") rather than a concluding idea.

The pictures support the text. For instance, the drawing that accompanies the writer's discussion about her rabbit chewing on the carpet includes a picture of the writer and her parent scolding the rabbit: "No!"

Score Point 3 *continued*

My rabbit is gray.

My rabbit is friendly.

My mom is sometimes

mad at my rabbit

because she chews the

carpet so we got a

bathroom mat for her

to chew on. My mom

Score Point 3 continued

Wos very happy.
Some rabbits have red
exes and some rabbits
have white exes just

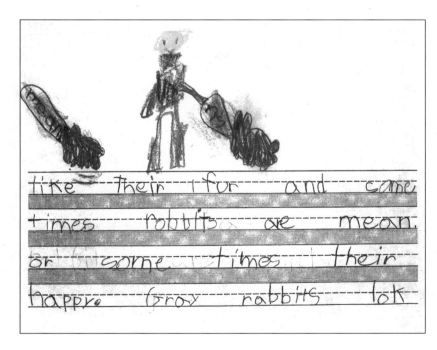

like their fur and some
times rabbits are mean.
or some times their
happy Gray rabbits lok

Score Point **3** *continued*

like ash and smoke.
Rabbits have good cense
of smelling. I like
rabbits because rabbits

are soft. There wiskers
help them sense and
it helps them. Rabbits
like carrots.

Assessment Summary: "The Rabbits Story"

ELEMENTS		
	Exceeds Standard	**Commentary**
Orientation and Context	• May announce the topic in the first sentence. • May rely on the title to announce the topic.	The writer relies only on the title to introduce the topic.
Organization of Information	• Produces and maintains a focus with an organizational structure (e.g., beginning, middle, end; chapters; circle structure).	Except for a narrative-like comment about the way her mother deals with their pet rabbit's tendency to chew on the carpet ("My mom is sometimes mad at my rabbit because she chews the carpet so we got a bathroom mat for her to chew on."), the writer shares information about her own rabbit, and rabbits in general, in the list-like structure that is typical of report at this age ("My rabbit is gray. My rabbit is friendly."). The details are not clustered by topic, but the piece has a general beginning, middle, and end.
Development and Specificity of Information	• Includes facts and information specific to the topic.	The piece includes specific details and a simile to describe rabbits of different colors and to provide details about rabbit anatomy ("Gray rabbits lok like ash and smoke."; "There wiskers help them sense and it helps Them."). The writer generalizes about rabbits by drawing on her own experience ("I like rabbits because rabbits are soft.").
Closure	• May include a simple concluding sentence.	The piece's final sentence is a statement about what rabbits eat ("Rabbits like carrots.") rather than a concluding idea.

STRATEGIES		
	Exceeds Standard	**Commentary**
Names and Vocabulary	• Uses common, everyday vocabulary.	
Other	• Pictures, if present, support the text.	The pictures support the text. For instance, the drawing that accompanies the writer's discussion about her rabbit chewing on the carpet includes a picture of the writer and her parent scolding the rabbit: "No!"

Note: The commentary highlights the elements and strategies in the student paper, focusing on how well the paper addresses the totality of the elements and strategies rather than on whether each is included.

Score Point 2

Report of Information Student Work and Commentary: "The Book abot Jelly-fish"

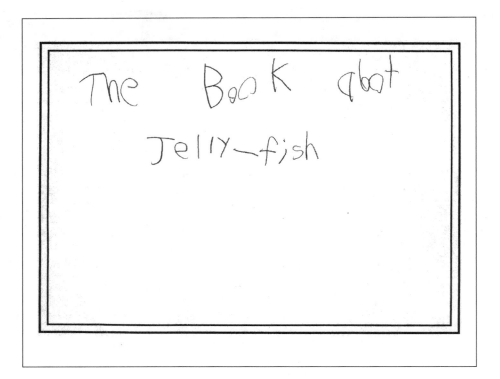

The Book abot Jelly-fish

"The Book abot Jelly-fish" is a good example of informational writing that meets the standard for kindergarten. The writer shares information about jellyfish with readers, and she stays focused throughout the piece.

The writer relies on the title of the piece to announce the topic for readers.

The writer shares information about the topic in a basic beginning-middle-end structure. Various facts about jellyfish are shared, but not clustered into groups. For instance, a fact about their anatomy ("Jellyfish have long stinging tentacles.") is followed by a fact about how long they have been on earth ("650 million years")

and a fact about how far they can swim ("Jellyfish can swim 3600 feet a day.").

In developing information about jellyfish, the writer uses specific details ("long stinging tentacles," "650 million years," "3600 feet").

The piece concludes with an evaluative statement ("Jellyfish are the best.") and a simple "the end."

For the most part (with the exception of drawings of her brother and herself), the pictures relate to the text in this piece. On the first page of her "book," she draws two jellyfish with long tentacles. On the second page, she labels another drawing to illustrate that jellyfish have "no brain."

Score Point 2 *continued*

Jellyfish have long stinging tentacles. Jellyfish have been on earth for 650 million years. Jellyfish can swim 360

Score Point 2 *continued*

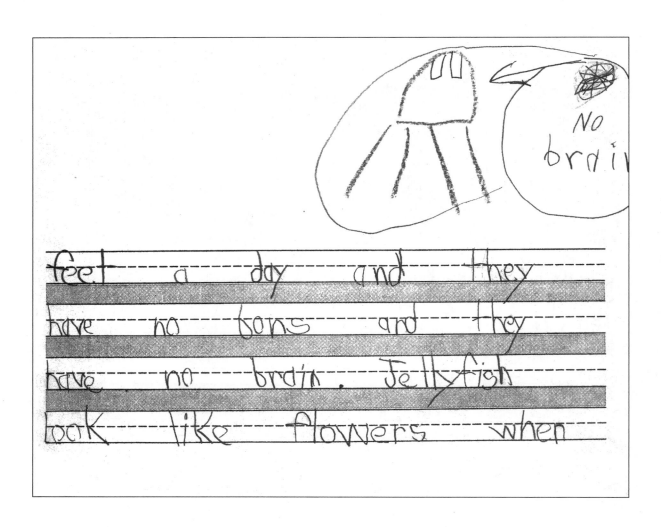

feet   a   day   and   they

have   no   bons   and   they

have   no   brain.   Jellyfish

look   like   flowers   when

Score Point 2 *continued*

they go to the bottom
of the sed. Jellyfish
are the best. the end

Score Point 2 continued

Assessment Summary: "The Book abot Jelly-fish"

ELEMENTS		
	Meets Standard	**Commentary**
Orientation and Context	• May announce the topic in the first sentence. • May rely on the title to announce the topic.	The writer relies on the title of the piece to announce the topic for readers.
Organization of Information	• Typically maintains a focus; stays on topic.	The writer shares information about the topic in a basic beginning-middle-end structure. Various facts about jellyfish are shared, but not clustered into groups. For instance, a fact about their anatomy ("Jellyfish have long stinging tentacles.") is followed by a fact about how long they have been on earth ("650 million years") and a fact about how far they can swim ("Jellyfish can swim 3600 feet a day.").
Development and Specificity of Information	• Includes facts and information specific to the topic.	In developing information about jellyfish, the writer uses specific details ("long stinging tentacles," "650 million years," "3600 feet").
Closure	• May include a simple concluding sentence.	The piece concludes with an evaluative statement ("Jellyfish are the best.") and a simple "the end."
STRATEGIES		
	Meets Standard	**Commentary**
Names and Vocabulary	• Uses common, everyday vocabulary.	
Other	• Pictures, if present, relate to the topic.	For the most part (with the exception of drawings of her brother and herself), the pictures relate to the text in this piece. On the first page of her "book," she draws two jellyfish with long tentacles. On the second page, she labels another drawing to illustrate that jellyfish have "no brain."

Note: The commentary highlights the elements and strategies in the student paper, focusing on how well the paper addresses the totality of the elements and strategies rather than on whether each is included.

Score Point 1

Report of Information Student Work and Commentary: "I read by My SeLf in The Living Room"

This kindergarten score point 1 paper is a report about the writer's reading habits. The paper shows early awareness of editing to stabilize spelling (for instance, in one place the letter "b" is crossed out and replaced with the letter "d"). Although this piece does not meet the standard, the writer's fluency is evident.

The first sentence announces the topic of the piece.

The organizing feature is a simple list of statements about reading.

The information provided has some detail: The writer uses a "red" book bag, has a favorite book (the "eara" book), and thinks that "IS NISe To read."

The concluding statement is a simple reflection ("I LiKe boocks").

Score Point 1 continued

I read by MY self in Te LIVINgRoom
I You z The red boock bag
do You No What is MY Favrit
boock is ? is MY Favrit
boock is The earabook.

iznise To read

I Like boocks
booooxc jk

Score Point 1 *continued*

Assessment Summary: "I read by My SeLf in The Living Room"

ELEMENTS		
	Approaching Standard	**Commentary**
Orientation and Context	• May announce the topic in the first sentence. • May not include a title.	The first sentence announces the topic of the piece.
Organization of Information	• May present information in a simple list.	The organizing feature is a simple list of statements about reading.
Development and Specificity of Information	• Makes some attempt to convey facts and information about the topic. • Provides few facts. • May include extraneous information.	The information provided has some detail: The writer uses a "red" book bag, has a favorite book (the "eara" book), and thinks that "IS NISe To read."
Closure	• May include a simple concluding sentence.	The concluding statement is a simple reflection ("I LiKe boocks").
STRATEGIES		
	Approaching Standard	**Commentary**
Names and Vocabulary	• Uses common, everyday vocabulary.	
Other	• Pictures, if present, may relate to the topic.	

Note: The commentary highlights the elements and strategies in the student paper, focusing on how well the paper addresses the totality of the elements and strategies rather than on whether each is included.

Next Steps in Instruction

The writer will benefit from working to increase fluency. She already knows how a stay with a topic, but does not generate enough text to be able to cluster ideas. The writer will also benefit from instruction on clustering ideas and adding information and detail. The list-like features of the piece suggest that a logical next step will be longer pieces.

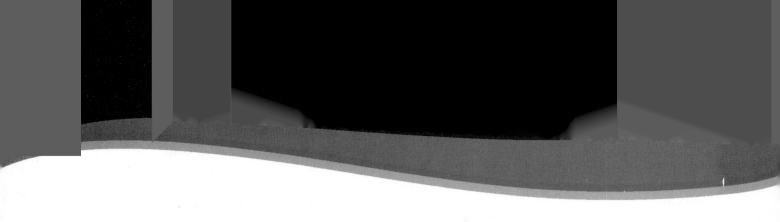

Instructions (sometimes called procedures, functional writing, or process essays) tell readers how to do something or describe how something is done through a sequence of actions. Beverly Derewianka (1990) explains that this genre is very important in our society because it makes it possible for us to get things done. There are many subgenres of this kind of writing: appliance manuals, science experiments, craft instructions, recipes, directions to reach a destination or to build a model, game rules, etc. In school, this type of writing appears frequently in science, homemaking, art, and other classes that focus on processes as opposed to things.

Instructions are like narratives because they are basically chronological in structure; however, instructions describe steps in a process instead of events in time. Because they are chronological in structure, children who write narratives can easily learn how to organize this genre. Young writers usually have little, if any, difficulty sequencing the steps in a plan of action.

Instructions require students to have expertise they can draw on. Fortunately, students have much expertise, even at the primary level. They know how to play games, care for pets, carve pumpkins, make peanut butter sandwiches, and so on. Having something to write about is not a problem for children who write this genre. However, the degree of specificity required sometimes makes writing instructions difficult, as does the problem of engaging the reader. Very young writers will sometimes adopt a narrative stance, presenting steps as actions they take or have taken ("I plant a sed [seed]. I water my sed [seed]. I wat far a rot [waited for a root]."). But when students see good examples of instructions, and model their own text on the examples, they are less likely to simply recount. Some topics are simply much more difficult for young writers than others. Topics that are too broad and/or detailed (for instance, how to play soccer, how to build a model car) are often too difficult for students, especially for those whose writing generally does not meet the standard.

Orientation and Context

There is no single way to begin instructions, but at the very least, writers must identify the activity or process and the goal. Writers of this genre also provide context, both in the beginning and throughout the text. They may explain why actions are necessary or why steps have to be taken in a particular order. They may include comments on the significance, usefulness, entertainment value, or danger of the activity in order to engage the reader. Typically, young writers of this genre also establish their credentials. That is, they create a knowledgeable stance. In texts by adult writers of this genre, a knowledgeable stance is often assumed. In the case of young writers, pictures may play a large role in providing both context and essential information.

Organization and Development of Instructions

Like narratives, instructions are organized by time. But instead of events, steps in a process or activity are the deep structure for organization. The text is organized by a sequence of actions. Typically, writers begin with the first step in the process and proceed in time until the last step. Goals are identified, materials are listed, typically in order of use, and steps oriented toward achieving the goal are described.

Writers elaborate on and organize steps in the process in a variety of ways (for example, by providing diagrams, giving reasons for actions, and creating visual imagery through words and illustrations). They create expectations through the use of predictable structures. Headings, subheadings, numbers, etc. are often used to make the process easy to understand and follow. Because instructions are organized by steps in time, common linking words are used (before, during, after, first of all, finally, next, later, simultaneously, subsequently, immediately following, in the meantime). Writers also use transition phrases to make their instructions clear and easy to follow ("When you're all done with that…"). The reader is typically referred to in a general way (one/you), but sometimes the reader is not mentioned at all if the writer uses commands to signal the steps to take ("Take the top off the hamster cage.").

When writing in this genre, successful writers provide a specific guide to action (or a specific description of the activity). They describe the steps or key components in detail, anticipating a reader's need for information and foreseeing likely points of confusion. They explain what to do, and how and why to do it ("Always try to give your hamster food at the same time each day. Then they can learn how to get up at the same time each day."). Sometimes they comment on who would need to know how to do the activity. They explain precautions that should be taken and warn about possible difficulties. They anticipate places where problems are likely to occur ("Food bowl heavy enough so the hamster can't pick it up"; "Don't give them citrus fruits, Onions, or garlic.").

Effective writers of this genre provide specific details (to explain how, what, where, and when), and they adjust the level of detail to fit the goal. They use diagrams or illustrations as complements and to supplement the verbal information in the text. They describe materials, tools, and preparations needed to carry out the process, providing precise information about size, length, weight, number, types, and so on. They define technical terms and explain steps in the process.

⊚Closure

Often the last step of the process is the conclusion of the writing. Although instructions may not always have a formal conclusion, writers typically provide some sort of closure. Sometimes writers explain the significance of the process or summarize the main steps. Young writers sometimes use a simple concluding statement to say how one could use the results if

the process leads to a product ("Maybe if you make enough you can sell them to people…"). Sometimes they simply exhort the reader to engage in the activity ("Now that you know something about Wakeboarding, get out their and wakeboard!").

Instructions in Kindergarten

Writers in kindergarten know how to do many things, and they delight in telling others how to do them. They know how to brush their teeth, make cookies, plant flowers, read books, and so on. But giving directions to others in writing offers new challenges for children, not the least of which are the challenges offered by the written mode. In addition to cracking the sound/print code, children must learn how to communicate with an audience who is not present. In face-to-face situations, participants can ask for clarification and point to objects in the environment ("Put that piece in the little hole there."). But instructions in writing need to contain more specific information because the reader of a written text is usually not present. Some children, especially those who have had little experience with written language, may initially find it difficult to anticipate the sort of detail a reader would need. Also, some children in kindergarten are just beginning to master the language conventions associated with giving instructions. When they attempt this kind of writing, very young writers may adopt a narrative stance. That is, they may describe the activity or procedure as something they have done or as actions being taken in the present ("I plant a sed [seed] I water my sed"). The sequence of steps may also be difficult to follow because the steps may not be ordered chronologically.

Writers who meet the standard at this grade level are able to tell someone what to do (for example, give instructions, send messages). They sequence steps in chronological order so that the reader can easily follow them. They may use simple temporal words to signal the sequence ("Frst"; "next"; "then"; "finally"). They fill in essential information that the reader will need ("frst you ned a big bll [bowl]"; "tcac sum eges [take some eggs]"). Some writers at this age use the title to introduce the topic. Others may draw a picture. They may provide closure with a simple evaluative statement about the activity ("It is fun.").

Note: It is quite likely that at kindergarten, the instructions that children write will be too general for anyone to follow ("tcac sum eggs [take some eggs]"), and it is also likely that important steps may be left out, as in the above example about planting a seed.

Instructions Rubrics Elements

	3 Exceeds Standard	2 Meets Standard	1 Approaching Standard
Orientation and Context	• Uses the title to introduce the topic.	• Uses the title to introduce the topic.	• Uses the title to introduce the topic.
Organization and Development of Instructions	• Provides a series of general steps or actions for carrying out a procedure or activity. • Organizes steps or actions in order by time. • Provides details that help the reader understand the instructions.	• Provides a series of general steps or actions for carrying out a procedure or activity. • Organizes steps or actions in order by time. • Provides some details that help readers understand the instructions.	• Presents a general series of steps or actions as simple commands or statements. • The reader may be unable to follow the sequence of steps or actions. • May omit important steps. • Provides few details. • May cast steps in past tense.
Closure	• Provides some sense of closure.	• May provide closure.	• May provide closure.

Instructions Rubrics Strategies

	3 Exceeds Standard	2 Meets Standard	1 Approaching Standard
Transition Devices	• Uses simple transition words to indicate the sequence of steps or actions (e.g., first, after, next) or numbers the steps. • May format the page to signal transitions between steps.	• Uses simple transition words to indicate the sequence of steps or actions (e.g., first, after, next) or numbers the steps. • May format the page to signal transitions between steps.	• May number the steps. • May attempt to format the page to signal transitions between steps.
Other	• May provide drawings to illustrate meaning.	• May provide drawings to illustrate meaning.	• May provide drawings in an attempt to illustrate meaning.

Score Point 3

Instructions Student Work and Commentary: "Haw to mac a cake"

In "Haw to mac a cake," the writer provides readers with a sense of the basic steps involved in making a cake. The piece exceeds the standard for writing instructions in kindergarten.

The title announces the topic for readers.

The piece includes a series of general steps for making a cake ("then you need to por the cak mix in." and "then you poot it in the uvin."). The steps are organized by time.

The piece includes important details, such as telling readers to "cac some eggs" instead of simply telling them to put eggs in the mix without mentioning that it is important to crack them.

The sentence "it is fun" gives the piece a sense of closure.

The piece includes simple transition words to help guide the reader through the process ("Frst," "then").

The writer illustrates the piece by including a drawing of a girl standing next to a large cake that is covered in candles. The piece also includes labeled drawings of the supplies she lists in the instructions (eggs, a bowl, and cake mix).

Score Point 3 *continued*

Score Point 3 continued

Assessment Summary:
"Haw to mac a cake"

ELEMENTS		
	Exceeds Standard	**Commentary**
Orientation and Context	• Uses the title to introduce the topic.	The title announces the topic for readers.
Organization and Development of Instructions	• Provides a series of general steps or actions for carrying out a procedure or activity. • Organizes steps or actions in order by time. • Provides details that help the reader understand the instructions.	The piece includes a series of general steps for making a cake ("then you need to por the cak mix in." and "then you poot it in the uvin."). The steps are organized by time. The piece includes important details, such as telling readers to "cac some eggs" instead of simply telling them to put eggs in the mix without mentioning that it is important to crack them.
Closure	• Provides some sense of closure.	The sentence "it is fun" gives the piece a sense of closure.

STRATEGIES		
	Exceeds Standard	**Commentary**
Transition Devices	• Uses simple transition words to indicate the sequence of steps or actions (e.g., first, after, next) or numbers the steps. • May format the page to signal transitions between steps.	The piece includes simple transition words to help guide the reader through the process ("Frst," "then").
Other	• May provide drawings to illustrate meaning.	The writer illustrates the piece by including a drawing of a girl standing next to a large cake that is covered in candles. The piece also includes labeled drawings of the supplies she lists in the instructions (eggs, a bowl, and cake mix).

Note: The commentary highlights the elements and strategies in the student paper, focusing on how well the paper addresses the totality of the elements and strategies rather than on whether each is included.

Score Point 2

Instructions Student Work and Commentary: "How to Get set for school"

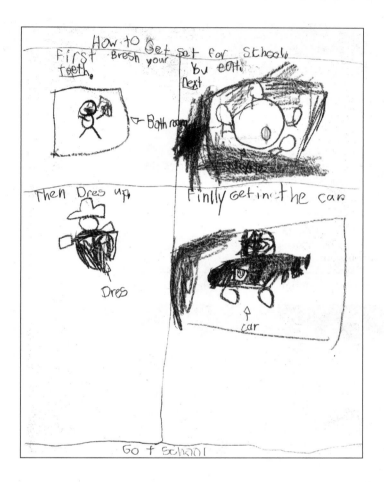

This piece of writing grows out of the writer's own experience, and it is obviously written student-to-student. The piece includes four general steps involved in getting ready for school, and it meets the standard for writing instructions in kindergarten.

The title introduces the topic.

The piece includes several general steps involved in getting ready in the morning ("First Bresh your Teeth.").

The writer includes a closing comment ("Go t school").

The writer uses simple transition words to help give the piece coherence ("First," "Finlly").

The writer places each step in a separate box, and the page layout helps guide the reader through the steps for getting ready for school.

The drawings that accompany each step illustrate the meaning. For instance, the step "First Bresh your Teeth" includes a picture of a girl brushing her teeth and the label "Bathroom."

Score Point 2 *continued*

Assessment Summary: "How to Get set for school"

ELEMENTS		
	Meets Standard	**Commentary**
Orientation and Context	• Uses the title to introduce the topic.	The title introduces the topic.
Organization and Development of Instructions	• Provides a series of general steps or actions for carrying out a procedure or activity. • Organizes steps or actions in order by time. • Provides some details that help readers understand the instructions.	The piece includes several general steps involved in getting ready in the morning ("First Bresh your Teeth.").
Closure	• May provide closure.	The writer includes a closing comment ("Go t school").
STRATEGIES		
	Meets Standard	**Commentary**
Transition Devices	• Uses simple transition words to indicate the sequence of steps or actions (e.g., first, after, next) or numbers the steps. • May format the page to signal transitions between steps.	The writer uses simple transition words to help give the piece coherence ("First," "Finlly"). The writer places each step in a separate box, and the page layout helps guide the reader through the steps for getting ready for school.
Other	• May provide drawings to illustrate meaning.	The drawings that accompany each step illustrate the meaning. For instance, the step "First Bresh your Teeth" includes a picture of a girl brushing her teeth and the label "Bathroom."

Note: The commentary highlights the elements and strategies in the student paper, focusing on how well the paper addresses the totality of the elements and strategies rather than on whether each is included.

Score Point 1

Instructions Student Work and Commentary: "I Plant a sed..."

This is a very early attempt at describing a procedure. The writer includes a series of four steps involved in planting a seed. This piece of writing approaches the standard for writing instructions in kindergarten. Like many early attempts at writing instructions, this piece is cast as a recounting—the writer tells how to do something by recounting the experience as if it is something she has done.

The writer presents each step as a simple statement about an action she has taken ("I Plant a sed I water my sed." and "I wat [wait] Far a rot [root].").

The writer presents a general series of actions, but it is difficult to follow the steps the writer outlines. For instance, the first step ("I Plant a sed") and the fourth step ("I Plant it") are the same.

The writer numbers her steps, and she organizes the steps spatially by dividing the scenes into four separate boxes.

She uses pictures to illustrate her meaning and add detail, and each step includes pictures with labels of the different items ("me," "rug," "table," "sun"). The labels demonstrate her attempt to incorporate her growing vocabulary into her writing by spelling words phonetically ("catlpter").

Score Point 1 *continued*

Score Point 1 *continued*

Assessment Summary: "I Plant a sed..."

ELEMENTS		
	Approaching Standard	**Commentary**
Orientation and Context	• Uses the title to introduce the topic.	The writer announces the topic in the first sentence ("I Plant a sed...").
Organization and Development of Instructions	• Presents a general series of steps or actions as simple commands or statements. • The reader may be unable to follow the sequence of steps or actions. • May omit important steps. • Provides few details. • May cast steps in past tense.	The writer presents each step as a simple statement about an action she has taken ("I Plant a sed I water my sed." and "I wat [wait] Far a rot [root]."). The writer presents a general series of actions, but it is difficult to follow the steps the writer outlines. For instance, the first step ("I Plant a sed") and the fourth step ("I Plant it") are the same.
Closure	• May provide closure.	The final step is "I Plant it."

STRATEGIES		
	Approaching Standard	**Commentary**
Transition Devices	• May number the steps. • May attempt to format the page to signal transitions between steps.	The writer numbers her steps, and she organizes the steps spatially by dividing the scenes into four separate boxes.
Other	• May provide drawings in an attempt to illustrate meaning.	She uses pictures to illustrate her meaning and add detail, and each step includes pictures with labels of the different items ("me," "rug," "table," "sun"). The labels demonstrate her attempt to incorporate her growing vocabulary into her writing by spelling words phonetically ("catlpter").

Note: The commentary highlights the elements and strategies in the student paper, focusing on how well the paper addresses the totality of the elements and strategies rather than on whether each is included.

Next Steps in Instruction

The writer will benefit from time and practice developing fluency. Instruction on introducing a topic to readers would also be helpful.

Response to Literature

The responding to literature genre assessed by New Standards is recognized and assessed in many districts and states throughout the United States, and like other genres, it provides a rough template that defines expectations for a particular kind of writing. But it is important to note that it is only one of several ways that readers and writers respond to literature and only one of several encouraged by teachers in school. Responding to literature can take many different forms. All of them are valuable in a language arts curriculum.

Students may respond in writing to literature in a variety of ways and for a variety of purposes—to express their emotional reactions, clarify their thinking or attitudes, explore difficulties in their understanding, or simply to share their opinions with others to build a social relationship. Teachers sometimes design classroom activities that invite informal, imaginative responses wherein the focus is on helping children make connections to their own experiences and to other texts or authors they have read. Such connections deepen children's understanding.

In the classroom, the development of more formal responses is supported both by these kinds of activities and by Accountable Talk[SM]. Accountable Talk offers a set of tools for helping teachers lead academically productive group discussions. Accountable Talk is not empty chatter; it seriously responds to and further develops what others say, whether the talk occurs one-on-one, in small groups, or with the whole class. When they engage in Accountable Talk, students learn to introduce and ask for knowledge that is accurate and relevant to the text under discussion. They learn to use evidence from the text in ways that are appropriate and follow established norms of good reasoning.

Built on this kind of scaffolding, formal written responses require students to examine texts thoughtfully and to draw evidence from them to make assertions and substantiate arguments. A good response to literature is never built on unsupported opinion. Polished and crafted for an audience, effective papers in this genre always demonstrate a comprehensive understanding of the work, and they persuade readers to accept the writer's interpretation and evaluation of a work of literature by providing evidence.

The New Standards expectations for responding to literature in writing center on this more formal, school-based genre. In the world outside of school, this genre is realized in published reviews of books, poetry, short stories, or other texts. Reviews are judged for the writer's ability to craft effective and defensible commentary—a coherent analysis that is supported by evidence.

The New Standards expectations for student writers in the response to literature genre require that student writers provide an introduction, demonstrate an understanding of the work, advance an interpretation and possibly an evaluation, include details from the literature that support the writer's assertions, use a range of appropriate strategies, and provide closure. Supporting judgments with evidence from the text is at the heart of this genre.

Orientation and Context

There are many ways to introduce a response to a literary work, depending upon the writer's purpose, but introductions usually share some common elements. Context is typically provided, such as the subject of the literature, the identity of the author(s), and the title(s) of the work or works that will be discussed. The writer may also attempt to engage the reader's interest by suggesting a reason for the reader to want to read the literature or by using an attention-grabbing lead. Some writers articulate the main point of their response in the introduction.

Comprehension, Interpretation, and Evaluation of Literature

The core of a response is the writer's interpretation and evaluation of the literature. Successful writers of this genre make assertions about the work that focus on the important elements of the text. They demonstrate comprehension of the work and a good grasp of the significant ideas of the work or passages in the work. They advance judgments that are interpretive, analytic, evaluative, or reflective, dealing with ambiguities and complexities in the text(s). They deal with questions about motivation, causality, and implications. They typically comment on the author's use of stylistic devices and show an appreciation of the effects created. They make perceptive judgments about the literary quality of the work.

Effective writers of this genre illustrate their interpretations or evaluations of the literature (for example, evaluations of an author's craft, interpretations of a work's theme) with examples or other information about the text. It is common for writers to summarize or paraphrase the work, or relevant parts of it, but successful writers of this genre do not simply retell. They make choices about what to tell the audience and what not to tell, depending upon the points they want to make.

Writers of this genre also sometimes compare and contrast the work they are responding to with other works that they have read or with their own life experiences. They may draw analogies between events or circumstances in literature and events or circumstances in their own lives. In other words, they connect the literature to their life experiences or culture. They support their interpretations or inferences by explaining the characters' motives or the causes of events based on their understanding of people and life in general. They often use quotations to explain and support their interpretation or to illustrate aspects of the author's craft. Used appropriately, quotations add to the credibility of the writer's conclusions.

Evidence

When students write a formal response to literature, they make a judgment about something they have read or have heard read to them. This judgment can be evaluative ("I liked it because…") or it can be interpretive ("I think the author is saying…"). Successful writers of this genre develop credible arguments to support their judgments. Significantly, this genre requires students to go back into the text to support their evaluation or interpretation. Although reader-response approaches stress the value of individual and unique encounters with text, reader-response theorists do not advocate the idea that every reading of a text is as good as any other. Louise Rosenblatt (1968) says that we must challenge students to be disciplined in the way they work with texts by (1) showing what in the text justifies their response and (2) making clear the criteria or standards of evaluation that they are using.

Because the deep structure of response to literature is argument, usually more than one assertion is put forward, and each is supported by evidence. Individual assertions add weight to the argument and relate back to the writer's overall interpretation or evaluation of the text. In order to make sense of the writer's interpretation or evaluation of a text, the audience needs adequate evidence—examples, details, quotations—along with explanations and reasons. Successful writers of this genre support their interpretations, inferences, and conclusions by referring to the text, other works, other authors, or to personal knowledge. They move beyond purely associative or emotional connections between the literature and their own experience (text-to-self connections) to explain how the connections they write about support their interpretations and evaluations. They convince the reader through logic and with evidence that is both sufficient and relevant. They typically use connecting words associated with reasoning (because, so, the first reason). If they are comparing works, they make accurate and perceptive observations of the similarities and differences between the works, and they support their observations by referring to the texts.

Successful writers of this genre express their feelings and reactions, but they do not overly rely on appeals to emotions or overstate their case. Although young children may often exaggerate or make sweeping generalizations, as they mature, their arguments are more often based on logic and reasoning. Successful writers of this genre do not make hasty generalizations marked by words like "all," "ever," "always," and "never." They qualify their claims, using words like "most," "many," "usually," and "seldom," when such words would be more accurate, and they support their opinions with evidence.

Closure

Although a response to literature may not always have a formal conclusion, writers typically provide some sort of closure, such as a summing up of the writer's perspective on the work. Writers of this genre often leave the reader with a fresh insight, a quotation, or some other memorable impression.

Response to Literature in Kindergarten

Students in kindergarten frequently give opinions about the books they have read. Typically, these are simple evaluative statements that convey their reactions and preferences. They react to characters ("I like the beby."), to authors ("I like Eric Carle."), to the book as a whole ("I like the book dous a kangiwo hav a muthri too?" [Does a Kangaroo Have a Mother, Too?]), and to the topic ("I like the Dolphin.").

Less advanced students may use a simple list structure of such reactions to develop and organize their writing ("I like the Dolphin. I like the beby."). They may not identify the book or story, and they may not provide closure. If they attempt retellings, their retellings are typically skeletal with few, if any, details.

At this grade level, students who meet the standard are able to get the gist of books they read independently; when responding to literature, they are able to create a written response that shows comprehension of the story. Typically, they provide a retelling of the storyline if the book is a narrative ("My favrit gidid reading book is roll over. The little one wisae [wished] to. Go on the bed and then they rolled over then he had a liltte spase [little space] and he wetied [wanted] more spase [space] one fell out in the ending he Had a lotse [lots] of spas [space] then he said goodnite."). To introduce the topic of their writing, students who meet the standard often announce the title of the book ("my fabit [favorite] book is do you want to be my friend."). Sometimes they refer to a particular event in the book ("I like when King Mixdes [Midas] cant [counted] his good [gold] he get sumoer [smaller]"). They provide closure to their writing, typically with a simple concluding statement ("You shID [should] eed [read] shIs [this] bk [book]"). They may also provide reflective comments about the book or particular incidents in it ("it mak me thek ubat [makes me think about] a uther soren [another story]...").

Response to Literature Rubrics Elements

	3 Exceeds Standard	2 Meets Standard	1 Approaching Standard
Orientation and Context	• May announce the title of the book. • May refer to an event in the story.	• May announce the title of the book. • May refer to an event in the story.	• May not identify the book or story.
Comprehension, Interpretation, and Evaluation of Literature	• Demonstrates an understanding of the gist of the work. • Usually provides an opinion or reflective comment about the book or the author (e.g., "it mak me thek ubat [make me think about] a uther soren [another story]...").	• Demonstrates an understanding of the gist of the work. • Usually provides an opinion or reflective comment about the book or the author (e.g., "I like the ho [whole] book"; "this rms [reminds] me of...").	• May demonstrate an understanding of the work. • May give a simple opinion about a character, the author, the book itself, or the topic (e.g., "I like..."; "my favrit [favorite]...").
Evidence	• Provides a relatively detailed retelling of the story line (or an overview of the information in the book).	• Provides a retelling of the story line (or an overview of the information in the book).	• May only provide a skeletal retelling (or overview of the topic). • May use a simple list structure (e.g., "I like Dolphin. I like the beby [baby].").
Closure	• Typically provides closure (e.g., "I thec [think] that som won [someone] shood red [should read] the caurrot [carrot] seed because it is a good store [story].").	• Typically provides closure (e.g., "You shID [should] eed [read] shls [this] bk [book].").	• Typically does not provide closure.

Response to Literature Rubrics Strategies

	3 Exceeds Standard	2 Meets Standard	1 Approaching Standard
Compare/ Contrast	• Usually refers to a single work. • May associate events in the work with events in his or her own life.	• Usually refers to a single work. • May associate events in the work with events in his or her own life.	• Usually refers to a single work. • Typically does not refer to events in his or her own life.
Other	• Typically does not mention literary techniques or concepts.	• Typically does not mention literary techniques or concepts.	• Typically does not mention literary techniques or concepts.

Score Point 3

Response to Literature Student Work and Commentary: "I like When King Mixdes..."

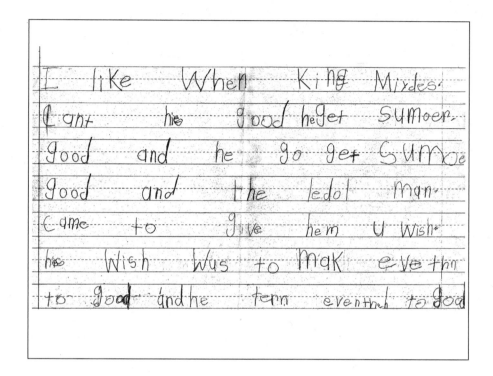

In this lengthy piece, the writer retells the King Midas story he has read and makes a connection between the book and another story. This piece exceeds the standard for a response to literature at kindergarten.

The writer introduces the topic by referring to an event in the story ("I like When King Mixdes Cant his good [gold] he get sumoer [some more].").

The writer includes a relatively detailed retelling of the story line, and the retelling demonstrates his understanding of the story ("the ledol man. came to give hem U wish his Wish Wus to MaK eVethn [everything] to good [gold] and he turn eventhen [everything] to good [gold]."; "then he tern the into food good [food into gold]"; "and he tern his DoDer [daughter] BaK to

nermol."). In the story, King Midas is so moved by greed that he turns everything around him into gold, including his daughter; when he realizes the mistake he has made, he must find a way to return things to their normal state. The writer's retelling of the story demonstrates that he understands it.

The piece includes a reflective comment that compares the King Midas story with another book ("thes maKs Me theK U Bat a uther soren [This makes me think about another story] and it Make Me theK Ubat the big JUP").

The writer closes by repeating the reflective comment ("it Mak Me tek U Bat U nuther soren [it makes me think about another story]").

Score Point 3 continued

King Midas tern has DoDer
and the King Midas wus sad
in to good and the
liden Man came to give good
to King Midas and he tern
the bed in to good
and then he tern
the in to food good.

and the lierd Man
came to mak eve thn
to henmoi he tern the
Frog bak to henmoi
and he tern the
YBriue ta hermol and
he tern his DoDer
Bak to menmoi.

Score Point 3 *continued*

and   thes   maks
Me   theK   u Bat   a
uther   soren   and
It   MaK   Me   theK
uBat   the   big   J uP
and   it   MaK   Me   teK
u Bat   u   nther   soren

Score Point **3** *continued*

Assessment Summary: "I like When King Mixdes..."

ELEMENTS		
	Exceeds Standard	**Commentary**
Orientation and Context	• May announce the title of the book. • May refer to an event in the story.	The writer introduces the topic by referring to an event in the story ("I like When King Mixdes Cant his good [gold] he get sumoer [some more].").
Comprehension, Interpretation, and Evaluation of Literature	• Demonstrates an understanding of the gist of the work. • Usually provides an opinion or reflective comment about the book or the author (e.g., "it mak me thek ubat [make me think about] a uther soren [another story]...").	The writer's retelling of the story line demonstrates that he understands it. The piece includes a reflective comment that compares the King Midas story with another book ("thes maKs Me theK U Bat a uther soren [This makes me think about another story] and it Make Me theK Ubat the big JUP").
Evidence	• Provides a relatively detailed retelling of the story line (or an overview of the information in the book).	The piece includes a relatively detailed retelling of the story line ("the ledol man. came to give hem U wish his Wish Wus to MaK eVethn [everything] to good [gold] and he turn eventhen [everything] to good [gold]."; "then he tern the into food good [food into gold]"; "and he tern his DoDer [daughter] BaK to nermol."). In the story, King Midas is so moved by greed that he turns everything around him into gold, including his daughter; when he realizes the mistake he has made, he must find a way to return things to their normal state. The writer's retelling of the story demonstrates that he understands it.
Closure	• Typically provides closure (e.g., "I thec [think] that som won [someone] shood red [should read] the caurrot [carrot] seed because it is a good store [story].").	The writer closes by repeating the reflective comment ("it Mak Me tek U Bat U nuther soren [it makes me think about another story]").
STRATEGIES		
	Exceeds Standard	**Commentary**
Compare/ Contrast	• Usually refers to a single work. • May associate events in the work with events in his or her own life.	
Other	• Typically does not mention literary techniques or concepts.	
Note: The commentary highlights the elements and strategies in the student paper, focusing on how well the paper addresses the totality of the elements and strategies rather than on whether each is included.		

Score Point 2

Response to Literature Student Work and Commentary: "I like the book dous a Kangiwo..."

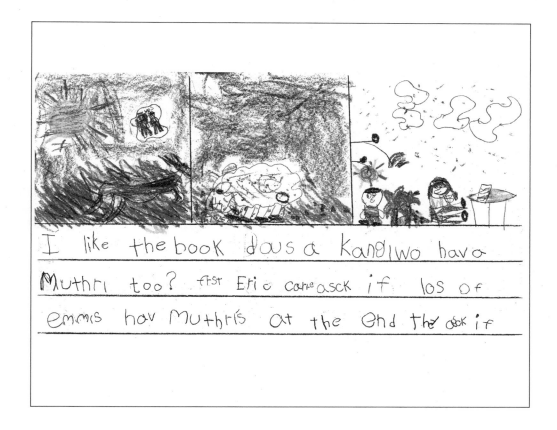

In this response to Eric Carle's *Does a Kangaroo Have a Mother, Too?*, the writer demonstrates an understanding of the gist of the work and makes a personal connection with the book. This piece meets the standard for a response to literature in kindergarten.

The writer begins by providing a reaction to the book ("I like the book dous a Kangiwo hae a Muthri too?").

The piece continues with a short retelling that discusses the beginning and end of the book ("frst Eric CarLe asck if los [lots] of emmis [animals] have Muthris [mothers] at the end they asck if ammi Muthrs [animal mothers] love ther babes."). The retelling demonstrates that the writer understands the gist of the book.

The piece includes a reflective comment about the book ("I like the hol book").

The writer makes a personal connection with the book in her response ("this remis me of weh I asck my mom WUS today."). The personal statement ends the piece.

Score Point 2 *continued*

dmm! Muthrs love ther babes. I like the hol book this tmis me of weh I asck my mom wus today.

Score Point 2 continued

Assessment Summary:
"I like the book dous a Kangiwo..."

ELEMENTS		
	Meets Standard	**Commentary**
Orientation and Context	• May announce the title of the book. • May refer to an event in the story.	The writer begins by providing a reaction to the book ("I like the book dous a Kangiwo hae a Muthri too?").
Comprehension, Interpretation, and Evaluation of Literature	• Demonstrates an understanding of the gist of the work. • Usually provides an opinion or reflective comment about the book or the author (e.g., "I like the ho [whole] book"; "this rms [reminds] me of...").	The writer's retelling demonstrates that she understands the gist of the book. The piece includes a reflective comment about the book ("I like the hol book").
Evidence	• Provides a retelling of the story line (or an overview of the information in the book).	The piece includes a short retelling that discusses the beginning and end of the book ("frst Eric CarLe asck if los [lots] of emmis [animals] have Muthris [mothers] at the end they asck if ammi Muthrs [animal mothers] love ther babes.").
Closure	• Typically provides closure (e.g., "You shID [should] eed [read] shIs [this] bk [book].").	The writer concludes by making a personal connection with the book ("this remis me of weh I asck my mom WUS today.").
STRATEGIES		
	Meets Standard	**Commentary**
Compare/ Contrast	• Usually refers to a single work. • May associate events in the work with events in his or her own life.	The writer makes a personal connection with the book ("this remis me of weh I asck my mom WUS today.").
Other	• Typically does not mention literary techniques or concepts.	
Note: The commentary highlights the elements and strategies in the student paper, focusing on how well the paper addresses the totality of the elements and strategies rather than on whether each is included.		

Score Point 1

Response to Literature Student Work and Commentary: "Eric Care likeS TO drAw A sun..."

The young writer of this piece has responded more to Eric Carle's art than to the text of his book(s). To some degree, this response makes sense because the artwork is central to all of Eric Carle's books. This piece approaches the standard for a response to literature in kindergarten.

The writer names the author (Eric Carle), but he does not identify the book or provide a retelling of it.

The writer gives an opinion about the author and the artwork ("Eric Care likes TO drAw A sun becaAUSe the Sun MAK hAM hAPPE").

Assessment Summary:
"Eric Care likeS TO drAw A sun..."

ELEMENTS		
	Approaching Standard	**Commentary**
Orientation and Context	• May not identify the book or story.	The writer names the author (Eric Carle), but he does not identify the book or provide a retelling of it.
Comprehension, Interpretation, and Evaluation of Literature	• May demonstrate an understanding of the gist of the work. • May give a simple opinion about a character, the author, the book itself, or the topic (e.g., "I like…"; "my favrit [favorite]…").	The writer gives an opinion about the author and the artwork ("Eric Care likes TO drAw A sun becaAUSe the Sun MAK hAM hAPPE"). The writer responds more to Eric Carle's art than to the text of his book(s). To some degree, this makes sense because the artwork is central to all of Eric Carle's books.
Evidence	• May only provide a skeletal retelling (or overview of the topic). • May use a simple list structure (e.g., "I like Dolphin. I like the beby [baby].").	
Closure	• Typically does not provide closure.	The piece simply stops.
STRATEGIES		
	Approaching Standard	**Commentary**
Compare/ Contrast	• Usually refers to a single work. • Typically does not refer to events in his or her own life.	
Other	• Typically does not mention literary techniques or concepts.	
Note: The commentary highlights the elements and strategies in the student paper, focusing on how well the paper addresses the totality of the elements and strategies rather than on whether each is included.		

Next Steps in Instruction

This student needs time to develop as a writer. He needs some oral guidance about how to respond to a book (questions such as "Did you like it? What was it about? What part did you like best? Why is that your favorite part?") before he attempts to answer these kinds of questions in writing.

Black, P., & Wiliam, D. (1998). Inside the black box: Raising standards through classroom assessment. *Phi Delta Kappan, 80*(2), 139–149.

Bruner, J. (1985). Narrative and paradigmatic modes of thought. In E. Eisner (Ed.), *Learning and teaching the ways of knowing* (pp. 97–115). Chicago: University of Chicago Press.

Cooper, C.R. (1999). What we know about genres, and how it can help us assign and evaluate writing. In C.R. Cooper & L. Odell (Eds.), *Evaluating writing: The role of teachers' knowledge about text, learning, and culture* (pp. 23–52). Urbana, IL: National Council of Teachers of English.

Derewianka, B. (1990). *Exploring how texts work*. Newtown, Australia: Primary English Teaching Association.

Hillocks, G., Jr. (1984). What works in teaching composition: A meta-analysis of experimental treatment studies. *American Journal of Education, 93*(1), 133–170.

Rosenblatt, L. (1968). A way of happening. *Educational Record, 49*, 339–346.